1948

Claude Shannon identifies the "bit" as a unit of digital information.

2016

Scientists at the University of Maryland create the first reprogrammable quantum computer.

1983

Microsoft introduces Word.

1945

Konrad Zuse develops Plankalkül, the first programming language.

1995

Brendan Eich develops the JavaScript language for the Internet age.

1957

John Backus leads a team that develops FORTRAN.

Anatomy of a Computer

All computers are made up of four basic parts: an input device, memory or storage, a processor, and an output device.

MEMORY/STORAGE. Data is stored here. It includes internal memory (the computer's hard disk) and external memory storage devices (for example, flash drives).

OUTPUT DEVICE. These show you the results of whatever the computer has processed. The screen, printer, video projector, and speaker are all output devices.

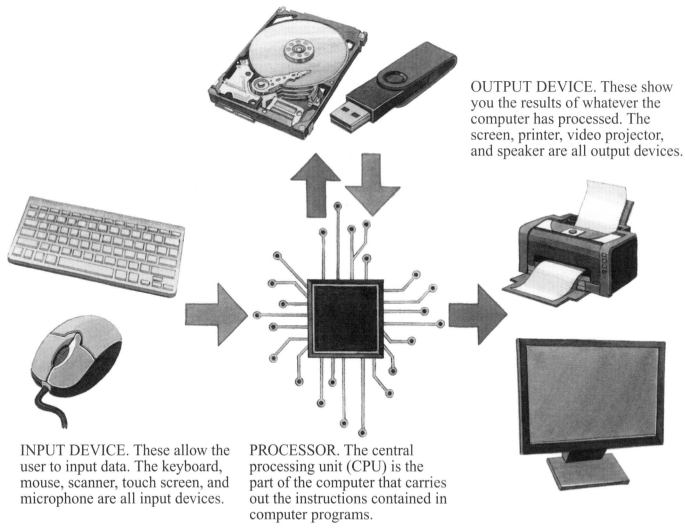

INPUT DEVICE. These allow the user to input data. The keyboard, mouse, scanner, touch screen, and microphone are all input devices.

PROCESSOR. The central processing unit (CPU) is the part of the computer that carries out the instructions contained in computer programs.

Author:

Alex Woolf studied history at Essex University, England. He is the author of over 60 books for children. They include *The Science of Natural Disasters*, *The Science of Rocks and Minerals*, and *You Wouldn't Want to Live Without Books!*

Artist:

David Antram was born in Brighton, England, in 1958. He studied at Eastbourne College of Art and then worked in advertising for 15 years before becoming a full-time artist. He has illustrated many children's nonfiction books.

Editor: Jonathan Ingoldby

Editorial Assistant: Mark Williams

PAPER FROM
SUSTAINABLE
FORESTS

Published in Great Britain in 2019 by
The Salariya Book Company Ltd
25 Marlborough Place, Brighton BN1 1UB

Library of Congress Cataloging-in-Publication Data
Names: Woolf, Alex, 1964- author. | Antram, David, 1958- illustrator.
Title: You wouldn't want to live without coding! / written by Alex Woolf ; illustrated by David Antram.
Description: New York : Franklin Watts, an Imprint of Scholastic Inc., [2018]
| Series: You wouldn't want to | Includes bibliographical references and index.
Identifiers: LCCN 2018014028| ISBN 9780531128121 (library binding) | ISBN 9780531193600 (pbk.)
Subjects: LCSH: Computer programming.
Classification: LCC QA76.6115 .W66 2018 | DDC 005.13--dc23 LC record available at https://lccn.loc.gov/2018014028

All rights reserved.
Published in 2019 in the United States
by Franklin Watts
An imprint of Scholastic Inc.

Printed and bound in China.
Printed on paper from sustainable sources.
1 2 3 4 5 6 7 8 9 10 R 28 27 26 25 24 23 22 21 20 19

SCHOLASTIC, FRANKLIN WATTS, and associated logos are trademarks and/or registered trademarks of Scholastic Inc.

Scholastic Inc., 557 Broadway, New York, NY 10012

You Wouldn't Want to Live Without™ Coding!

Written by
Alex Woolf

Illustrated by
David Antram

Series created by
David Salariya

Franklin Watts®
An Imprint of Scholastic Inc.

Contents

Introduction   5

How Do You Code a Computer?   6

How Did Coding Begin?   8

Who Invented the First Computers?   10

How Did Computers Develop?   12

What Are Programming Languages?   14

How Has the Internet Affected Coding?   16

Who Creates Computer Programs?   18

What Is Debugging?   20

What Is Hacking?   22

What Is a Computer Virus?   24

How Does Coding Help Us?   26

What Is the Future of Coding?   28

Glossary   30

Index   32

Introduction

Without coding, all the computers in the world would be useless boxes of plastic and metal. You could feed information into them, but they wouldn't know what to do with it. Coding means creating a set of instructions (or algorithm) that tells a computer how to perform a task. Another word for coding is *programming*. When you think about how much we rely on computers in our daily lives, you start to realize the importance of coding. Computers are used not only in smartphones and laptops, but also in kitchen appliances, traffic lights, heating systems, elevators, and cars. The world would certainly be a much less comfortable and convenient place without coding.

How Do You Code a Computer?

Writing code means telling a computer what to do. This is a challenge because computers really only understand two kinds of data: on and off. Every computer contains billions of tiny devices called transistors. These are switches regulating the flow of an electric current, and they are either on or off. "On" can be represented as "1," and "off" as "0." This system of ones and zeros is known as binary code, and it's the most basic of computer languages. But to write a computer program in binary code would take years. So we use programming languages. These do the work of translating the programmer's instructions into binary code.

I'm sorry, can you say that to me in binary?

Running a Program

/* Hello, World program */
#include<stdio.
h> main() {
print ("Hello,
World");

This is how source code looks in a programming language called "C."

How do you count in binary? Unlike decimal, there are just two digits: 1 and 0. Yet both systems follow the same pattern: When you run out of digits, place 1 in the column to the left, and 0 in the right-hand column. In decimal, 9 is followed by 10. In binary, 1 is followed by 10.

1	1
2	10
3	11
4	100
5	101
6	110
7	111
8	1000
9	1001
10	1010

1. SOURCE CODE. Say you want to instruct a computer to print "Hello, World." First, you write the instruction in "source code," which uses words humans can read. Source code can be used on many different computers.

2. ASSEMBLY LANGUAGE. A program called a compiler translates source code into assembly language, which uses a combination of words and numbers to represent binary code. Assembly language is specific to a particular type of computer.

3. MACHINE CODE. The computer sends the assembly language to a program called an assembler, which converts it into machine code. Now the instructions are presented in binary, and the computer can understand and execute them.

BYTES. Binary code is grouped into bytes—groups of eight binary digits (bits). A byte is the smallest unit of digital data. A letter of the alphabet, for example, would be represented as a byte. A million bytes is a megabyte. A billion bytes is a gigabyte.

How Did Coding Begin?

Basile Bouchon was a weaver living in Lyon, France, in the early 1700s. In those days, weavers had to spend a long time setting up their looms to produce each new weaving pattern. In 1725, Bouchon had the idea of automating this process using paper with holes punched into it. A cylinder rotated the paper, bringing a fresh pattern of holes into line with a row of hooks on the loom. If a hook met a hole, the thread would not be raised; if a hook met paper, the thread would be raised. The raised and lowered threads created the pattern. The paper tape was a kind of early program—a set of instructions controlling the loom.

Now he's just showing off.

DRUM MACHINE. In 1206, Arabic inventor al-Jazari wrote a book describing 100 mechanical devices. One was a musical band with a drummer robot that could be programmed to play different rhythms—perhaps the earliest example of coding.

In the early 1900s, automated "player pianos" became popular. Air sucked through a hole in a paper roll would open a valve, causing a wooden finger to strike a note. The holes would be arranged to play a popular tune.

It's the future, I tell you!

The weavers won't like it.

BINARY MARBLES. In the 1670s, Wilhelm Leibniz imagined a calculating machine in which binary numbers were represented by marbles. A punched card system would allow the marbles to fall into channels if they met a hole in the card.

PUNCHED CARDS. Jacques de Vaucanson (1709–1782) improved Bouchon's loom by replacing the roll of paper with punched cards. The presence or absence of holes determined the patterns woven by the loom. His idea was ignored in his lifetime, however.

JACQUARD LOOM. In 1804, Joseph Marie Jacquard (1752–1834) improved Bouchon's and de Vaucanson's ideas to create the Jacquard loom. It revolutionized the weaving industry, and weavers were angry, thinking the loom would put them out of work.

Who Invented the First Computers?

harles Babbage was an English mathematician who, in 1837, designed (though never built) the first mechanical computer, the Analytical Engine. Inspired by the Jacquard loom, he planned to program his machine using punched cards. He was assisted by the mathematician Ada Lovelace. In 1842–1843, Lovelace created an algorithm for the Analytical Engine to compute a sequence of numbers. Many experts regard this as the first computer program. Lovelace foresaw that computers could be used for more than mathematical calculations and could compute any logical problem.

This will be a great calculating engine!

It could be more than that.

IN 1886 HERMAN HOLLERITH developed a machine for compiling statistics. Data was recorded as holes on punched cards, so it could be sorted and counted automatically. Hollerith got his idea from watching a railroad conductor punch tickets.

Early computers used vacuum tubes rather than transistors as switching devices. Vacuum tubes are glass tubes emptied of air, containing electrodes that control the flow of an electric current. ENIAC had over 17,000 such tubes. But their unreliability limited the capability of early computers.

ALAN TURING, a pioneer of computer science, created in 1936 a theoretical computer, the Turing Machine. It could read, write, and manipulate symbols on a strip of tape, according to a table of rules. His machine would have unlimited memory, so it needed an infinite amount of tape.

THE ATANASOFF-BERRY COMPUTER, built in 1939, could solve just one kind of mathematical equation, and couldn't be reprogrammed to do anything else.

ENIAC, built 1943–1945, was one of the earliest computers that could be reprogrammed. It could perform calculations a thousand times faster than any machine of the time and covered 1,830 square feet (170 square meters).

How Did Computers Develop?

The first computers were huge and slow, but in 1947 a team of scientists invented the transistor, a tiny electronic switch that was fast and reliable. It quickly replaced the vacuum tube. In 1958, Jack Kilby invented the computer chip, integrating all the components of an electric circuit onto a piece of germanium. Computers could now be much smaller, and mass-produced. The 1970s saw the arrival of the personal computer (PC). In the 1980s, PCs became more user-friendly. In the 1990s, they were linked up through the World Wide Web. By the 2000s, smartphones had appeared, and were millions of times more powerful than the biggest early computers.

> Today's smartphones are more powerful than the computers that put humans on the moon.

> And he just plays games on it.

> I think we're getting too smart.

> Blame Moore's Law.

MOORE'S LAW. In 1965, businessman and scientist Gordon Moore predicted that the number of transistors on a computer chip would double about every two years. His prediction proved accurate until 2012, when the rate began to slow.

AHEAD OF HIS TIME. In 1968, US inventor Douglas Engelbart gave a live demonstration of linked computers, windows, graphics, the computer mouse, and video conferencing many years before these things became a reality.

> Doesn't look like a mouse!

A computer chip performs three basic functions:
1. It performs mathematical operations like addition and multiplication.
2. It moves data from one memory location to another.
3. It makes decisions and jumps to a new set of instructions based on those decisions.

They wouldn't want to live without me.

That's what they said about me once.

FLOPPY DISK. In 1971, a team of engineers invented the "floppy disk." This enabled data to be shared between computers. Until the 1990s, floppy disks were the main way of storing and exchanging computer data.

THE FIRST successful PC was the Altair 8800 (1975). This was a kit that had to be put together. The early PCs were soon followed by the first software for games, word processing, and spreadsheets.

DESKTOP PUBLISHING. In the mid-1980s, desktop computers appeared with graphical user interfaces (icons and drop-down menus) and design software so users could create professional-looking documents.

What Are Programming Languages?

Coding for early computers was done in assembly language, a "low-level" language very close to machine code. It was a long, painstaking process, and errors were unavoidable. As computers became more powerful, programmers needed higher-level languages, closer to human language. If high-level languages had never been developed, today's computers would be very slow and full of "bugs." Being human-readable, high-level languages are easy to learn and can be used across a range of computers. Popular high-level languages include Python, C, Ruby, JavaScript, and PHP.

FORTRAN, one of the earliest high-level programming languages, was developed by John Backus in 1957. At first, programmers were skeptical about it because it used human words. However, FORTRAN proved to be a great success, and versions of it are still in use today.

FLOW-MATIC. In the late 1950s, computer scientist Grace Hopper noticed many business people struggling with the mathematical symbols needed when using computers. So she wrote FLOW-MATIC, the first programming language to express computer operations in natural language.

BASIC, developed in 1963, was a simple progamming language. In 1975, Bill Gates (above left) and Paul Allen (above right), founders of Microsoft, used BASIC to write software for the Altair 8800.

OOP (object-oriented programming), developed in the 1980s, meant code could be broken down into a sequence of "objects," making coding easier. Code became like a smartphone: no need to know what was in it, only what it did.

Top Tip

How to learn a programming language:
1. Choose an appropriate language for your needs.
2. Install any necessary software. Most languages need "compilers" to translate your code into machine code.
3. Learn the language's syntax (rules defining how to set out words and symbols).
4. Start with a simple exercise such as printing "Hello, World."

Help! Python!

Don't worry, that's one of the easier languages.

15

How Has the Internet Affected Coding?

im Berners-Lee is a British computer scientist and founder of the World Wide Web. In 1989, when he had his big idea, the Internet already existed on a small scale, but the Web would make it easier for computers around the world to link up, and for people to search for and share information. In 1990, he wrote the software that enabled this to happen. The rapid growth of the Internet since then has had a huge impact on coding. In the Internet age, programming languages have had to be flexible, high-level, and easy to learn.

Coding was much harder in my day!

SCRIPTING LANGUAGES. The Internet led to a need for scripting languages. Easy to write, they contain their commands within files that can be converted directly into machine code while the program is running.

CONFUSION! At first, the Internet was a confusing place. It had lots of information, but no easy way of finding it. It was like having a phone but no one's phone number. So coders developed the first search engines.

You wouldn't want to live without search engines!

Top Tip

How to use a search engine:
1. Input only the keywords. Too few keywords may get you too many results. Too many keywords might get you no results.
2. Put quote marks around a set of words to find an exact phrase.
3. Add a minus symbol (-) before a word to exclude pages with that word.

PYTHON "PROGRAMMING LANGUAGE" -SNAKE

No, I don't want a pull-along duck!

PAGERANK. One of the key pieces of coding in the history of the Internet was an algorithm to rank websites in a search engine. PageRank (1996) uses a mathematical formula to measure the importance of web pages based on the number and quality of links to them from other pages.

YOU MAY ALSO LIKE . . . Websites watch what we buy and use this data to suggest related items that might interest us. This is all done using algorithms, and can lead to mistakes. For example, if you buy a toy for your three-year-old cousin, it might suggest something similar for you!

Who Creates Computer Programs?

The people who write the code for our computers are called programmers. Some create the operating systems that make these devices run. Others create apps (software for games and other programs). First, programmers identify the needs of users. Then they design and write programs to fulfill those needs. Once a program is written, they run tests on it to find any errors ("bugs") to ensure it runs smoothly. After a program has been launched, programmers monitor it, making updates as needed.

Can I borrow some code?

No, we only lend books.

SHORT CUTS. Programmers often use libraries of existing code that they can modify. This makes programs more reliable and with fewer bugs.

Is there an app for that?

Clean your room!

MOBILE APPS. People building apps for smartphones and tablets face particular challenges: Text and images must be visible on a small screen; the app must be interactive, using touch-screen technology; and it must be easily navigable.

You're not a complex character, are you?

VIDEO GAME DESIGNERS first develop the concept, setting, characters, and story, then work with artists to create the look and programmers to write the code. Games can be very complex, with millions of lines of code needed to create just one character.

???

WHY USE PROGRAMMERS? Why can't we program computers using natural language? Because it's inexact. When speaking we use words, idioms, and metaphors that would confuse a computer. That's why we wouldn't want to live without programmers.

18

What Is Debugging?

On September 9, 1947, in Virginia, computer pioneer Grace Hopper and her team encountered an error on their Harvard Mark II computer. They investigated and found a moth had gotten caught in the machine. The moth was removed and taped to a logbook. Beneath it Hopper wrote, "First actual case of bug being found." This was the world's first "computer bug." Soon people were talking of "debugging" computers, meaning fixing errors in a program. The famous moth, by the way, can still be seen displayed at the Smithsonian Museum in Washington, D.C.

Where are you, Logical Bug?

Logical Bug

Syntax Bug

COMPUTER PROGRAMS are made up of millions of lines of code, so it's not surprising that programmers sometimes make mistakes and introduce bugs. There are two types of bugs: syntax bugs and logical bugs. Syntax bugs are easy to spot. Logical bugs are harder to find.

How It Works

The debugging process begins as soon as a program has been written. Programmers can use a "debugging tool," a program that goes through every line of code, testing it for errors. You wouldn't want to live without a debugging tool!

Come on, chase me!

Help!

SYNTAX BUGS occur when a programmer mistypes a piece of code, preventing the computer from carrying out a command. So, in a game in which your character is supposed to be chased around the screen by an evil rabbit, if the evil rabbit doesn't move, this is probably due to a syntax bug.

LOGICAL BUGS happen when the programmer hasn't mistyped anything, but has made an error with the logic. The program still works, but in a different way than intended. In this case, the evil rabbit chases after you, but when you try to hide, it always finds you.

MISSING A STEP can cause problems. Programs are a set of instructions, like a recipe. For example, "bake chocolate brownies for 30 minutes, then serve" doesn't say to take the brownies out of the oven! That would cause a logical bug.

A SEMANTIC ERROR is when there's a problem with the meaning. An example of a semantic error in natural language would be the sentence "Chocolate brownies dream of evil rabbits." It's grammatically correct, but it doesn't make sense!

What Is Hacking?

In 1943–1944, René Carmille worked for the National Statistics Service in Nazi-occupied France. He altered the population census by reprogramming a punched-card computer, saving untold numbers of French Jews from the Nazi death camps. He was the world's first computer hacker—someone who gains unauthorized access to a computer to perform actions the creator or user never intended. Many of today's hackers are criminals. They hack into computers to steal people's money, personal information, or identity.

HACKERS enjoy the challenge of breaking into an organization's security system. The public generally views them as villains, but many hackers see themselves as playing a positive role in pointing out flaws in computer security.

Hacking into tomorrow's test was too easy!

Top Tip

To avoid being hacked, be suspicious of emails: Sometimes criminals mimic an organization you know and ask you to update your personal information. Don't! Encrypted sites (where you see "https" in the web address) are the safest ones to visit. Always choose difficult-to-guess passwords.

It's dark gray, all right?

HATS. Like cowboys in a Western movie, hackers are classified by hat. "White hats" are "good" hackers who work for companies, testing their security software. "Black hats" are criminals who hack for personal gain. "Gray hats" hack into security systems, but for fun, not profit.

FINDING FLAWS. You wouldn't want to live without the white hats! Good hackers help prevent major crimes like cyberterrorism and identity theft.

You need us!

HACKTIVISTS. People known as hacktivists hack into computer systems to bring about political or social change. For example, some hacktivists are motivated by a belief that secret government information should be released to the public.

What Is a Computer Virus?

n 1982, a 15-year-old high-school student created a computer game for his friends. Hidden inside the game was a program that was released the 50th time they played it. Instead of playing the game, the screen would display a poem. This was one of the earliest computer viruses. A computer virus is a program designed to infect a computer and alter the way it operates. This virus was a harmless prank, and it came on a floppy disk. These days, viruses often do real damage to computers, and they spread easily from one computer to another, much like a flu virus.

DAMAGE. Viruses can damage a computer's operating system, and corrupt or erase data. They can steal passwords and personal information, record keystrokes, and even take over a computer completely.

A VIRUS works by inserting itself into, or attaching itself to, a normal program. Viruses can lie dormant for long periods on a computer, until the infected program is opened. The virus will then execute its code.

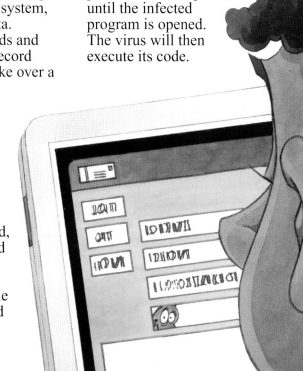

SPREADING. In today's connected world, computer viruses spread very easily through email and text message attachments, Internet file and app downloads, and social media links.

Top Tip

You wouldn't want to be without antivirus software. This is software used to prevent, detect, and remove computer viruses. Make sure you have it installed on your devices, and keep it updated with the latest version.

BE CAREFUL. People who spread viruses are crafty. They will often hide them in appealing or amusing content that people like to share. Never download files or open links or attachments unless you trust the source.

How Does Coding Help Us?

Today, coding is everywhere, and you wouldn't want to live without it! Computer apps help us stay in touch, stay fit, learn, shop, get around, and entertain ourselves. To really appreciate the impact of coding on our lives, we'd need to step back to an earlier era, like the 1970s. In those days, to listen to music, you had to go to a store and buy it on vinyl or tape. To write anything, you used a pen or a typewriter. Books, newspapers, and TV were the main sources of information. There were no apps to help you find your way around—only printed maps.

MAKING CONNECTIONS. Computer programs have created an entirely new way of doing business, by bringing people together who can help each other. If Susan wants to rent out a room, and Maria needs a place to stay, there's an app to put the two of them in touch.

Imagine getting all these facts at the touch of a button.

PERSONALIZED LEARNING. Today, teachers in some schools in the United States are using apps to design personalized learning plans for their students. These digital teaching programs explain topics in math and English at a pace the student is comfortable with.

How It Works

Computer programs are used to generate visual content, from movie special effects to video games. With computer-generated imagery (CGI), realistic scenes are created by building geometric models of objects. "Ray tracing" simulates the way light acts on an object's surface to make it appear 3-D.

Check out my CGI fur!

Now you're dreaming, son.

PATIENT MONITORING. In hospitals, computers monitor patients' blood pressure, pulse, and oxygen levels. They are programmed to notify the staff if any of these vital signs move out of normal ranges.

MAKING MUSIC. Today, many musicians compose with the aid of a computer. Pieces of software called plug-ins are used to add new sounds from "virtual instruments" to enhance the piece.

What Is the Future of Coding?

The coding revolution may only be just beginning. Algorithms are becoming increasingly sophisticated, and this has led to a rise in machine learning, or artificial intelligence (AI). Computers are no longer just labor-saving devices. Already they are helping us make important decisions, working side by side with teachers and doctors, piloting probes in outer space, translating foreign languages, conversing with us, and beating us at games like chess. And they're likely to become even more intelligent in the future.

AUTOMATED TRAVEL. Self-driving vehicles are being tested, and will soon come into widespread use. The technology isn't perfect yet: While humans can recognize an icy patch on a road, this sort of thing is difficult to build into an algorithm.

SMART HOMES. Software will soon be embedded in many parts of our homes. Your house plants will know when they need watering, and will tell you. Your alarm clock will not only wake you, but alert your coffee maker to start brewing.

CYBORGS. In the future, people may be able to get implants to communicate with one another, or even watch movies! Amputees may be fitted with prosthetic limbs that receive signals from the brain to give them greater control of movements.

How It Works

We can converse with voice-activated assistants on our devices, thanks to voice recognition software. The AI doesn't try to understand every word, but looks for keywords and interprets our meaning that way. It learns through experience, so it's always improving.

What is it?

I think it's called non-artificial intelligence.

DANGEROUS JOBS. Today, human-directed robots are used to defuse bombs and do dangerous jobs in mining and industry. As AI improves, these robots will be able to act with increasing autonomy, making their own decisions, free of human control.

EMOTIONS. Some scientists believe the brain is a sophisticated computer, and that emotions like love are algorithms that can ultimately be broken down into zeros and ones. They believe that one day we'll be able to program robots to feel genuine emotion.

I love you.

But do you mean it?

Glossary

Algorithm A set of rules to be followed by a computer. Computer programs are algorithms.

App Short for "software application," this is a self-contained computer program designed for a particular purpose.

Assembly language A low-level programming language that can be converted into machine code by an assembler.

Binary code A coding system in which binary numbers (zeros and ones) are used to program a digital computer.

Bug An error in a computer program.

Byte A group of eight binary digits, used as a unit of memory size.

Chip Short for "microchip," this is a wafer of material (usually silicon) containing a large number of tiny transistors. Chips perform calculations, move data, and follow programmed instructions.

Compiler Software that translates code written in one programming language into another language.

Cyberterrorism Using computers to cause disruption or fear for political reasons.

Download Copy data from one device to another, usually over the Internet.

Floppy disk A flexible magnetic disk inside a hard plastic case used for storing data from a computer.

Hacking Gaining unauthorized access to data on a computer, often in order to perform actions the computer's creator or user never intended.

Internet A global network of computers, allowing international communication, data transfer, and information sharing.

Machine code The most basic kind of programming language consisting of binary instructions that a computer can respond to directly.

Memory The part of a computer where data or program instructions can be stored for retrieval.

Plug-in Software that is added to a computer system to give extra features or functions.

Search engine A program that searches for and identifies items in a database that match keywords specified by the program's user. Search engines are regularly used to find particular sites on the World Wide Web.

Software The programs and operating systems used by a computer. This contrasts with a computer's hardware, which is its physical components.

Source code A list of commands, usually in human-readable text, to be assembled into a computer program.

Spreadsheet An electronic document in which data is arranged in rows and columns and can be manipulated and used in calculations.

Statistics The collecting and analyzing of large quantities of numerical data.

Syntax The structure of statements in a computer programming language.

Transistor A tiny device that can amplify or switch an electronic signal. Modern microchips contain up to 7 billion transistors.

Vacuum tube A sealed glass tube containing a near-vacuum (airless space) through which an electric current can pass freely.

Virus A piece of code hidden within, or attached to, a computer program that can corrupt or destroy data, and transfer itself to other computers.

Website A location on the Internet that maintains one or more web pages.

World Wide Web An information system on the Internet that allows documents to be connected to other documents by special links, enabling users to search for information.

Index

A
al-Jazari 8
algorithms 5, 10, 17, 28, 29
Altair 8800 13, 14
Analytical Engine 10
antivirus software 25
apps 18, 24, 26, 27
artificial intelligence (AI) 28–29
assembly language 7, 14
Atanasoff-Berry Computer 11

B
Babbage, Charles 10
Berners-Lee, Tim 16
binary code 6, 7
Bouchon, Basile 8, 9
bugs 18, 20–21

C
Carmille, René 22
compilers 7, 15
computer chips 12, 13
computer-generated imagery
  (CGI) 27

D
debugging tools 20, 21
desktop publishing 13

E
Engelbart, Douglas 12
ENIAC 11

F
floppy disks 13, 24

G
games 13, 18, 19

H
hackers 22–23
Hollerith, Herman 11
Hopper, Grace 14, 20

I
Internet 16–17, 24

J
Jacquard, Joseph Marie 9
Jacquard loom 9, 10

L
Leibniz, Wilhelm 9
logical bugs 21
Lovelace, Ada 10

M
machine code 7, 14, 15, 16
Moore's Law 12

O
object-oriented programming 15
operating systems 18, 24

P
PageRank 17
personal computers (PCs) 12, 13
player pianos 9
plug-ins 27
programmers 18–19

programming languages 6, 7,|
  14–15, 16, 19
  BASIC 14
  C 7, 14
  FLOW-MATIC 14
  FORTRAN 14
  JavaScript 14, 19
  PHP 14, 19
  Python 14, 15
punched cards 9, 10, 11, 22

R
robots 29

S
scripting languages 16
search engines 17
security, computer 23, 25
self-driving vehicles 28
semantic errors 21
smartphones 5, 12, 18
source code 7
syntax bugs 21

T
transistors 6, 11, 12
Turing, Alan 11

V
vacuum tubes 11, 12
Vaucanson, Jacques de 9
viruses, computer 24–25

W
World Wide Web 12, 16

Top Computer Programmers

1. Ada Lovelace (1815–1852) published the first computer algorithm and was the first to realize that computers had uses beyond pure calculation.

2. Grace Hopper (1906–1992) pioneered high-level computer programming languages, inspiring the creation of COBOL, still used today.

3. Donald Knuth (1938–) worked out formal mathematical techniques for computer algorithms and wrote the "bible" of coding, *The Art of Computer Programming*.

4. Dennis Ritchie (1941–2011) created the influential C programming language and co-created the Unix operating system.

5. Ken Thompson (1943–) created the B programming language and co-created the Unix operating system.

6. Bjarne Stroustrup (1950–) created and developed the widely used C++ programming language.

7. Tim Berners-Lee (1955–) invented the World Wide Web and developed the essential algorithms that enabled it to work.

8. Bill Gates (1955–) co-created (with Paul Allen) Microsoft, the world's biggest PC software company.

9. Guido van Rossum (1956–) created the Python language.

10. Linus Torvalds (1969–) created the Linux kernel, the program at the core of the Linux, Android, and Chrome operating systems.

Computer Vision

Computers are extremely good at solving logical problems like math and chess. They find it much harder to understand visual information. Because our ancestors spent millions of years using their eyes to find food or evade predators, we have become extremely good at pattern recognition—identifying objects. But to a computer, existing in a world of zeros and ones, even figuring out where an object ends and a background begins can be difficult.

What Is a Dog?

Think about how easy you find it to recognize that both a poodle and a Great Dane are dogs. It would take a lot of complex coding to teach a computer that these animals belong to the same species. In 2012, it was big news when a computer managed to identify pictures of cats with almost 75 percent accuracy.